Wales

History of Religion, Pre-Christian Wales

Author

Kelvin Gordon

Copyright Notice

Copyright © 2017 Global Print Digital
All Rights Reserved

Digital Management Copyright Notice. This Title is not in public domain, it is copyrighted to the original author, and being published by **Global Print Digital**. No other means of reproducing this title is accepted, and none of its content is editable, neither right to commercialize it is accepted, except with the consent of the author or authorized distributor. You must purchase this Title from a vendor who's right is given to sell it, other sources of purchase are not accepted, and accountable for an action against. We are happy that you understood, and being guided by these terms as you proceed. Thank you

First Printing: 2017.

ISBN: 978-1-912483-23-5

Publisher: Global Print Digital.
Arlington Row, Bibury, Cirencester GL7 5ND
Gloucester
United Kingdom.
Website: www.homeworkoffer.com

Table of Content

INTRODUCTION 1
ROMANS & THE COMING OF CHRISTIANITY 6
THE AGE OF THE SAINTS 10
THE NORMAN THREAT 17
PRINCES & BISHOPS 22
REFORMATION AND DISSOLUTION 26
CIVIL WAR 31
THE BIRTH OF NONCONFORMITY 35
HYMNWRITERS AND PREACHERS 39
THE BIRTH OF NONCONFORMITY 44
INDUSTRIALISATION & TEMPERANCE 48
CULTURE & POLITICS 53
THE REVIVAL 58
THE GROWTH OF SECULARISM 64
MULTICULTURAL WALES 70

Introduction
Pre-Christian Wales
Before Christianity arrived in Wales, archaeological evidence shows the existence of a variety of religious beliefs and rituals.

Evidence of the existence of the pre-historic peoples of Wales is to be found all over the country, literally on the ground as well as under it, and much of this relates to the burial of human remains.

Many sites have similar characteristics, making a strong case for the existence of a common belief system throughout the area during various periods, particularly when dealing with death. Perhaps this is why pre-historic religions have such a morbid image - for example the popular images of bloodthirsty

Druidic sacrifices. Evidence of rituals for marriages and births is not so widespread, or has yet to be identified as such.

One of the earliest burial sites was found at a cave on the Gower coast. Known as the Red Lady of Paviland, the skeleton actually belongs to a young man and dates from about 25,000 years ago. It is one of the oldest ceremonial burials found in western Europe. Buried alongside the remains was jewellery made from ivory and sea shells, and a mammoth's skull. The red ochre discovered on the remains suggests a symbolic link with blood, and there is a theory that the young man was a shaman, or a witch doctor figure.

Following the end of the last Ice Age some 10,000 years ago, people returned to what is now Wales. The period up to the Bronze Age, around 4,000 years ago, was the time that saw the building of dolmens and stone circles across the western fringes of

Europe. A dolmen, or cromlech, is a prehistoric megalith typically having two or three upright stones and a capstone. They are thought to be burial chambers and according to historians they are the earliest permanent structures built by people, older than the pyramids of Egypt. There are around 150 dolmens in Wales, the most notable being at Pentre Ifan in Preseli, Pembrokeshire.

Pembrokeshire also has a link with the most famous stone circle in Britain, Stonehenge, as its inner circle consists of bluestones, apparently from the same Preseli hills as where Pentre Ifan is situated. And Pembrokeshire's own ancient stone circle is to be found in the same area at Gors Fawr, near Crymych. There are numerous others across Wales.

These circles are believed to have been places for religious rituals, but no records survive of what actually went on.

This tradition of erecting stone circles was revived following the activities of 18th century antiquarian Iolo Morgannwg. It became a part of the activities of the National Eisteddfod, and to the present day wherever the Eisteddfod visits a stone circle is erected, and is the focus of Bardic ceremonies during Eisteddfod week. This is partly why people think the ancient Druids worshipped at these stone circles.

The introduction of metal working to Wales, combined with a change of climate, seems to have had an effect on the religious practices of the native people. For a start they stopped erecting dolmens and stone circles. The making of metal was believed to be an act of magic in itself, and many objects were made from this precious substance in its various forms - bronze and iron as well the more precious varieties of gold, silver and copper.

These objects seem to have become the basis of a religion based on their being given as offerings to the gods. Various metal objects dating from this period, from weapons to domestic utensils, have been discovered at the bottom of ancient lakes, such as Llyn Cerrig Fach and Llyn Fawr.

The religious leaders of these rituals became known as the Druids. We know a little more about them than their predecessors because they were around when the Roman Empire was expanding into north western Europe, a period relatively well documented. Julius Caesar wrote of Druids during his wars with the Gauls, and the historian Tacitus describes graphically the invasion of the Druidic stronghold of Anglesey, or Mona, in 60 AD.

The raid on Anglesey effectively marked the end of Druidism as an effective force in Britain, but worship of their gods was tolerated under the Roman regime.

Romans & the coming of Christianity

The Romans invasion of Britain in 43 AD brought new influences, and their own gods were combined with native British gods to produce religious hybrids. It also paved the way for a new religion which eventually overpowered the old pagan ways.

The old Druidic order was smashed in 60 AD when its stronghold of Anglesey was invaded by the Roman army. The Druids were the religious officials of the native Britons and they appear to have been the prominent force in fermenting anti-Roman sentiment. The invasion of Anglesey is an explicit acknowledgement of the threat they posed to Roman rule.

Druidism was a religion which may have originated in Britain. In Welsh the word for Druid is Derwydd, which is closely related to the Welsh for oak tree - derwen. And Welsh is a language directly descended from the Brythonic language spoken by the Britons at the time of the Roman conquest.

Julius Caesar noted that the Druids worshipped in oak groves, and according to the historian Tacitus, one of the first things the Roman invaders of Anglesey did was to cut down the many oak groves they found dotted all over the island.

Although Druidic political power was destroyed, worship of the native gods continued. The Roman attitude to religion appears to have been pragmatic - if it didn't threaten the Roman presence it was tolerated. Also they appear to have believed that it wasn't worth risking incurring the wrath of the native gods, for they would only experience bad fortune during their stay in this foreign land. So they got around it by trying to have the best of both worlds by pairing off their Roman gods with their British equivalents, and erecting joint shrines.

One of the most famous in Britain is to be found at the old Roman baths at Bath. The Romans built their shrine around the hot springs there in 54 AD, on the site of a much earlier temple built by the Britons. The original native goddess was named Sul and she was combined with her Roman equivalent Minerva to create the 'composite deity' Sulis Minerva.

In Wales an example of a 'composite deity' was found in temple dedicated to Mars-Oculus at Caerwent, and a stone head dating from around 300 AD found at Caerleon suggests that native British beliefs continued without having to combine with Roman practices.

Folk memories of these ancient British gods persist to the present day in the form of myths and legends, with the finest example in Wales being the Mabinogi. This collection of tales is thought to have been ancient by the time it was written down in the mid-eleventh century. Some believe it is the closest we can get to the magical world of the ancient Britons.

Around the same time as the stone head was being made in the early fourth century, two men named Aaron and Julius were executed in the very same town of Caerleon for following a proscribed religion. It is not known how many shared their fate. But within a hundred years this persecuted faith became the official religion of the Roman empire, and over time Aaron and Julius were acknowledged as the first Welsh Christian martyrs.

The age of the saints

Although initially banned, Christianity became the official religion of the Roman Empire. The empire's collapse in Britain created a 'Welsh' people whose identity has traditionally been based on Christianity and a common language.

Christianity arrived in Wales at the height of Roman power and was banned initially by the authorities who were suspicious of its secrecy and exclusivity. At first it was an urban religion, and the first Christian martyrs in Wales were killed early in the fourth century at the legionnaires' town of Caerleon.

However it soon became tolerated. The earliest Christian object found in Wales is a vessel with the ancient Christian symbol the Chi-Rho, dated 375 AD and found in the nearby Roman town of Caerwent. By the end of the 4th century Christianity became the sole official religion of the Roman Empire.

Gradually Roman power declined in Britain, until finally in 410 AD Emperor Honorarius advised the Britons to organise their own defences against the Barbarian threat. The only account to survive from this period comes from the Welsh cleric St Gildas.

Gildas wrote of the decline and ruin of Britain caused by its debauched and decadent rulers, with the pagan invaders being God's revenge for their spectacular fall from grace. The conflict, particularly with the Anglo-Saxons, created a process during the next two hundred years whereby a 'Welsh' people emerged out of the remaining Romano-Britons and native peoples, with their identity being chiefly based on a common religion and a common language.

By the time of St Augustine's mission in 597 AD to convert the Germanic tribes of south eastern Britain,

Christianity was long established in Wales and other parts of western Britain, such as Cumbria and Cornwall. The earliest Welsh poetry dates from just before St Augustine set foot on Britain, and the poems of Taliesin and Aneirin's Gododdin bear testimony to the fact that Christianity was by then long established amongst the native British.

This period is usually called the 'Age of the Saints', a time of intense Christian activity in western and northern Britain and Ireland. Probably the most famous 'Welsh' missionary is St patrick, who began the conversion of the Irish people. Ireland would later send out its own missionaries all over western Europe, and Patrick became acknowledged as the patron saint of the island.

In Wales St David, (Dewi Sant), became the pre-eminent Christian figure. He is the only native born patron saint of the countries of Britain and Ireland, a fact which speaks for the deep roots of Welsh

Christianity by the time of his birth around the early sixth century. Before David there were other Christian figures in Wales such as St Dyfrig and St Illtud. They were followed by St Teilo, St Padarn and St Deiniol as well as St David.

Little is known about these people, but they must have been very influential because they gave their names to various places all over Wales, pre-fixed by the word Llan. For example: St Illtud - Llanilltud Fawr (Llantwit Major), St David/Dewi Sant - Llanddewi, St Padarn - Llanbadarn, St Teilo - Llandeilo. 'Llan' is an old Welsh word thought to refer to an enclosure of land, which early Christians needed to consecrate for burials as well as building a cell or church for worship.

Those who inspired such activity had the enclosure named after them. Many of these places are reputed y situated at older, pagan sites of worship, such as wells. There are literally hundreds of place names in Wales beginning with 'Llan', attesting to the industry of these early Christians. As well as place names, other evidence of the activities of the early Welsh Christians are the hundreds of standing stones to be found all over the country with Christian related carvings or inscriptions on them. Some carry bilingual inscriptions in Latin and Ogham, which arrived in Wales with Irish settlers at the end of the Roman Empire. Others have intricate carvings which have become characteristic of the Celtic identity, such as the cross at St Brynach's church in Nevern, Pembrokeshire.

Little remains in the way of illustrated manuscripts from Wales to compare with the wonderful designs to be found in the Book of Kells and the Lindisfarne Gospels, although it is believed that the Gospel of St Chad may have Welsh origins. It did spend some time in Wales at some time in its history, although it has been at its present location of Lichfield for hundreds of years. As well as two evangelist portraits of St

Mark and St Luke, in its margins are found some of the earliest writings in Welsh, dating from the 9th century.

The eventual conversion of the Germanic tribes of England did not lead to a unifying of the Christian peoples of Britain under one organisation - which was the intention of the Papal mission led by St Augustine. Indeed, his approaches to Welsh bishops were firmly rebuffed in two meetings in 602 and 604 AD. Understandably the Welsh may have been unwilling to cooperate with a people which had disinherited them of the island of Britain, even if they had become Christian.

Later, there is evidence that Welsh and English Christians did find common ground as both nations came under attack from pagan Vikings from the late 8th century onwards. After dealing with the Danes in the late 9th century the great Saxon king Alfred set about improving learning in the English church, which had declined after years of attacks. He recruited a monk named Asser from the St David's monastery in west Wales. Asser became a close confidant of the king and his 'Life of King Alfred' is proof of the high standard of Latin used in the Welsh church. It is also an invaluable historical document on the life of a medieval English king.

It took Viking attacks to bring Welsh and English Christians closer together. It was to take the descendants of the Vikings, the Normans, to bring the Welsh at the point of a sword under the authority of the Archbishop of Canterbury.

The Norman threat

With the Pope's blessing King William conquered England in 1066, and he permitted Norman lords to raid Wales and carve out feudal lordships. These new masters also set about reforming the Welsh church.

Following his seizure of the English crown, William the Conqueror's Norman lords established bases along the Welsh border from where they carried out raids into Wales.

They found a country still in dynastic disarray after the death in 1063 of the Welsh high king Gruffudd ap Llywelyn. In 1081 William visited St David's, ostensibly to show his respects but in reality as a demonstration of his power to the native rulers.

Treaties were negotiated but the gloves came off after William's death in 1087.

In the absence of a restraining power on the English throne, independent Norman lords started carving out mini-kingdoms in Wales. First to go were Brecon and Pembroke, followed by Glamorgan. Before the end of the 11th century Norman presences were established in west Wales thanks to their special weapon, the castle. It appears that the Welsh were about to suffer the same fate as the English and go under the Norman yoke.

With the Normans hammering on the door, the Welsh church responded by producing works such as the 'Life of St David'. This was written by Rhigyfarch, son of Bishop Sulien, at the Welsh monastery in Llanbadarn, near Aberystwyth, in around 1090. The intention was to resist the intrusive influence of Canterbury which followed hard on the heels of the Norman attacks.

Written some 600 years after St David's death, many of the stories in the 'Life' are standard religious mythology, but there is enough biographical detail to show that David was a seminal figure in Welsh Christianity. Indeed, it may have led to his canonisation by Pope Callistus II in 1123, making him the only 'official' Welsh saint from the 'Age of the Saints'.

The new Norman rulers came face to face with a Welsh church which still retained many of its ancient characteristics. A number of the larger churches began life as native monasteries or clasau, often set within circular churchyards, whilst some of the smaller ones were first established as dependent chapels of a mother church, or as the private chapel of a local Welsh lord or noble.

Much of organised Welsh Christian tradition baffled the new bosses, such as a lack of dioceses with properly geographically-defined boundaries, and the tradition of priests marrying and raising families to serve in the church. The Normans introduced territorially defined dioceses, but their attempt to enforce clerical celibacy was not totally successful and cases of married priests with families lasted down to the Reformation.

These religious reforms were another means of tightening the Norman grip. The first bishop to swear an oath of allegiance to the archbishop of Canterbury was Urban of Llandaf in 1107, and by the middle of the century all Welsh bishops had followed suit. Another example of these reforms was the introduction of continental monasteries. The monastic order most closely associated with Norman rule was that established by St Benedict. And just as the first Norman castle in Wales was built at Chepstow in 1067, so its first Benedictine monastery was also built at Chepstow in 1071.

In the middle of the 12th century another monastic order from France, the Cistercians, came to Wales. Within some 30 years of their arrival the 'White Monks', unlike the Benedectines, had 'gone native', a situation which had real consequences for future Norman ambitions to conquer Wales.

Princes & Bishops

The Church became a pawn in the struggle between the native Princes and the Marcher lords. Edward I ended Welsh independence in 1282, although the Glyndwr uprising threatened Canterbury's supremacy.

Following the death of Henry I in 1135 England entered a period of disorder. This provided an opportunity for the native Welsh princes such as Rhys ap Gruffudd of Deheubarth to regain lost ground. Later known as The Lord Rhys, military success and political ability saw Rhys acknowledged as the pre-eminent native ruler of the twelfth century. His support of the Cistercians was an important development in the secular and religious life of medieval Wales.

The Cistercians came alongside other monastic orders to Wales as part of the development of Norman rule. As well as providing spiritual backup for Norman authority, they were also a means of developing the economy in Wales - indeed, they are credited with pioneering the Welsh woollen industry.

However, following the patronage of The Lord Rhys they were soon taken up by other Welsh rulers. By the end of the twelfth century they had gone 'native' and were very supportive of the aims of the Welsh rulers and Welsh culture.

The leading Welsh cleric of the age was Gerald of Wales (Giraldus Cambrensis), who shared descent with The Lord Rhys from the ancient kings of Deheubarth. Gerald more closely identified with Norman rule, although he was sympathetic to some aspects of Welsh independence, particularly in church matters. In the late 12th century his campaign to elevate St David's to an archbishopric was frustrated by Canterbury, yet he remains an important figure thanks to his writings about religion and politics in Wales and Ireland.

By the 13th century only the rulers of Gwynedd were called Princes. Under the leadership of Llywelyn I and his grandson Llywelyn II, the campaign to establish an independent Welsh principality was dealt a fatal blow by the death of Llywelyn II at Cilmeri in mid Wales in December 1282. His headless body was buried by Cistercian monks at Abbey Cwm-hir in mid Wales.

The end of political independence brought the church in Wales firmly under the rule of Canterbury. During the 14th century Welsh clerics were to complain bitterly that the best jobs in the Welsh church were given to English clerics, and that much of its revenue went east of Offa's Dyke.

This clerical frustration fed into the Glyndwr uprising of 1400 to 1410. Amongst Glyndwr's supporters were prominent churchmen like John Trefor, bishop of St Asaph. Dynastic disputes over the English crown and a schism in the Papacy were the background to the war.

The campaign was to acquire an international dimension thanks to the efforts of such supporters, yet, despite heroic efforts, hopes for Welsh independence were to be dashed and Canterbury's dominance reasserted.

Within a hundred years the Tudor dynasty would possess the English throne. Boasting Welsh ancestry (and a Glyndwr connection), their reign saw the end of the Roman Catholic Church in Wales as well as fundamental changes in the way the country was governed.

Reformation and dissolution

The foundation of the Tudor dynasty. Under Henry VIII Wales and England left the Roman Catholic Church, and one consequence was the translation of the Bible into Welsh.

The Battle of Bosworth in 1485 effectively marked the end of the dynastic conflict in England, popularly known as the Wars of the Roses. Following his victory, Pembroke-born Henry Tudor became King Henry VII. Some Welsh individuals gained from this change, and Welsh clergy were promoted to positions previously closed to them.

Henry VIII succeeded his father, and his quarrel with the Pope over his wish to divorce in order to marry Anne Boleyn eventually led to England and Wales leaving the Roman Catholic Church.

The dispute took place during the birth of the Protestant Reformation in Europe. While Henry did not become a Protestant, in asserting his authority over the Pope in his kingdom, some of the measures taken were influenced by these new ideas.

The monasteries were the first victims of this change. They had been in decline for many years, and their closure by government order caused little or no protest. The land and contents were sold off, with the profit going to the king. The buildings were stripped and left to the mercy of the elements.

This freeing up of land formerly owned by the monasteries gave new opportunities for ambitious members of the Welsh gentry to increase their estates. Owning land could be a complicated business for a Welshman due to old Welsh property law dating back to the tenth century king, Hywel Dda . Many Welsh nobles petitioned for the right to literally become 'English' and be governed by English law. Such tendencies coincided with the wider Tudor concerns of enforcing administrative uniformity throughout the kingdom in the face of possible threats from anti Reformation forces on the continent.

These were the underlying currents leading to the Acts of Union of 1536 and 1542 which abolished the remaining Marcher Lordships and incorporated Wales into England. Wales was given representation in Parliament, with the Welsh granted equal rights with the English, and what was left of original Welsh law was abolished. One side effect was that English was made the sole 'official' language throughout Wales.

Many of the gentry who gained from the dissolution of the monasteries remained Catholics. As the Protestant Reformation progressed in Wales and England under the Tudor dynasty, except during Mary's reign, Catholics began to face persecution. In Wales one poet's response was to label the new order 'ffydd Saeson' - 'faith of Saxons', and there was a strong feeling that the Welsh were being forced to abandon the old religion due to English demands.

A number of Welsh Catholics were to be martyred, although many embraced their fate joyfully. At Tyburn the Welsh priest Edward Morgan was reproved by a minister on the scaffold for being too cheerful at the prospect of going to heaven.

There were Catholics who passively resisted the changes by staying away from the new church services. Legislation was passed which punished these non-attenders, and they were called 'Recusants', a term which also was applied to some of the early Protestant dissenters. They faced substantial fines for non-attendance as well as incurring the suspicion of the authorities.

Most Welsh people seemed to have accepted these changes, although they probably mourned the banning of colourful religious events like pilgrimages under the new regime. But it was the translating of the Bible into Welsh during Elizabeth I's reign which enabled their eventual transformation into a Protestant people.

Making the Word of God understandable to the people was a very important part of the Protestant Reformation. A result of this was the emergence of differing opinions on the role of a monarch in a Christian society. As Charles I was to find out, the consequence in his case was to be quite literally fatal.

Civil War

The Civil War ended with Charles I's execution and the establishment of a Protestant Republic, but the Restoration saw various Protestant sects persecuted. In Wales the Quakers in particular were to suffer.

The lead up to the Civil War of the 1640s is woven with issues relating to politics, economic and social change, and religion. The rise in literacy following the translation of the Bible into the vernacular language helped the spread of new ideas in England, and some of these in turn spread into the border areas of Wales.

Bristol was a very influential centre of early Nonconformity, and it is no coincidence that the first

Nonconformist chapel in Wales was founded by Congregationalists in Llanvaches, Monmouthshire, in 1639, near the border with England.

Dissatisfaction with the reign of Charles I found a home within the emerging Puritan movement, which ultimately led to regime change and the previously unthinkable - the legal execution of the King of England in 1649 followed by the establishment of a Protestant Republic led by Oliver Cromwell.

One of the first acts of the Puritan regime was the passing in 1650 of the Act for the Better Propagation and Preaching of the Gospel . During the war Wales had been almost entirely Royalist, confirming the puritan view of Wales being a 'dark corner', and here the Act was applied to root out dissident clergymen. Radnorshire born Vavasor Powell came to prominence as a particularly enthusiastic, and feared, enforcer of this new law.

However, the Act also created new schools which taught children to read and write, although their work was hampered by the insistence on using English as the sole medium of instruction. Wales was still largely monoglot Welsh speaking at the time.

Within a couple of years of Cromwell's death in 1658 the monarchy returned to Britain. The Restoration was accompanied by a series of legal measures against Nonconformist sects which became known as the 'Clarendon Code'.

In Wales the Quakers in Montgomeryshire became the targets of persecution. One of the most famous cases involved the Lloyds of Dolobran, a prominent and much respected old family. Members were thrown into jail as a consequence of their beliefs. Some Quakers responded by moving to the American colonies in search of religious tolerance, and became prominent members of the Quaker community in America.

Another Protestant sect which had members fleeing to America at this time were the Baptists. John Miles was the founder of the first Baptist congregation at Ilston, Gower , in 1649. During the 1650s he built on this success, establishing chapels elsewhere across south Wales as well as being to official positions, yet the Restoration brought this progress to an abrupt end. The chapels withered away and John Miles was to end his days in a town he founded in Rhode Island called Swansey.

The end of the decade saw the 'Glorious Revolution' of 1689 when the Protestant monarchs William and Mary took the throne, and the Bill of Rights Act, which ushered in an era of religious toleration.

The birth of nonconformity

Religious freedom for dissent was accompanied by a steady rise in literacy, which prepared the way for massive changes.

The Toleration Act of 1689 finally allowed religious freedom to the hard core of Dissenters who had come into existence during the time of Oliver Cromwell. They defiantly adhered to their beliefs during the years of persecution following the restoration.

The first chapels in Wales were built during this period, with one of the most famous examples being Maes-yr-Onnen near Glasbury, Powys.

Much of the development of Dissent was possible because of the steady rise in literacy. This was given a boost by the 1650 Act for the Better Propagation and Preaching of the Gospel. Before the Toleration Act there were increasing numbers of religious books available. In Welsh, notable books published during the 1680s were Canwyll y Cymry ('The Welshman's Candle') by the Vicar Prichard, and the first Welsh translation of 'The Pilgrim's Progress' by John Bunyan. The last work in particular was to be very influential on prominent figures in the Methodist revival later in the 18th century.

Educational opportunities were growing in this period thanks to the work of bodies like the Welsh Trust . Set up by Thomas Gouge following an illegal preaching tour of Wales in 1671, the Trust endeavoured to tackle the disturbing levels of illiteracy and general destitution then existing.

Initially working in English, following the influence of Puritan Stephen Hughes, the Trust made available Welsh translations of the Catechism, the book of Psalms and the Book of Common Prayer. This was made possible due to the financial patronage of, amongst others, the Lord Mayor of London.

However the Trust was active for only a short time. Soon a new body was established to carry on the work, to be known as the Society for the Promotion of Christian Knowledge. The SPCK faced a serious problem with the shortage of teachers for its schools, a problem compounded by the fact that the teaching was in the medium of English whilst the majority of pupils were first language Welsh speakers.

Griffith Jones was a Welsh clergyman working for the SPCK who became very dissatisfied with the sole use of English in the important cause of saving Welsh souls, and he decided to do something about it. With the help of Carmarthenshire heiress and philanthropist Madam Bevan he set up circulating schools to teach elementary reading and writing skills. These schools were very successful in making a large section of the Welsh people literate. Established in the early 1730s, it has been estimated that the schools succeeded in teaching some 200,000 people basic reading and writing skills, out of an approximate population of some 450,000.

After Griffith Jones' death in 1761 Madam Bevan ensured the continuation of the schools. The Empress of Russia, Catherine the Great, was sufficiently impressed by the results of these schools to commission a report in 1764.

This increase in literacy undoubtedly helped pave the way for the momentous events of the latter part of the 18th century, when Wales experienced the Methodist Revival.

Hymnwriters and preachers

The beginning of the Methodist Revival in Wales and the first wave of great Welsh preachers and hymnwriters.

There were three great figures associated with what has become known as the Methodist Revival in Wales: Howel Harris (1714-73), Daniel Rowland (1713-90), and William Williams Pantycelyn (1717-1791).

Harris and Rowland both experienced, separately, a religious conversion in 1735, but they weren't to actually meet until 1737, when they decided to coordinate their evangelising activities - that date marks the effective beginning of the Methodist Revival in Wales.

All three were greatly influenced by the work and preaching of Griffith Jones of Llanddowror, and undoubtedly his Sunday Schools and the increase in literacy greatly contributed to the development of Methodism. Jones himself never embraced Methodism although he admitted to having some sympathy with its aims.

Methodism started off as a movement within the Church of England, with revival as its intention. Much influenced by what was happening in England, it went on to develop along different lines in Wales.

Howel Harris experienced his conversion during a sermon at the church in Talgarth in Breconshire and immediately began holding religious meetings at home. Soon he was preaching the gospel in the surrounding areas and before long all over Wales. A man of prodigious energy as well as passion, he often preached five sermons a day, sometimes encountering a hostile and violent response; however, his perseverance led to thousands being converted.

A man of strong opinions, his earnest beliefs led to a split with the other leaders of Welsh Methodism in the early 1750s. As a consequence he established a religious community at his home village of Trefeca. Before his death he was reconciled with Daniel Rowland and the movement, and William Williams composed an elegy noting his enormous contribution.

Howel Harris was never ordained in the Church of England, unlike his colleague Daniel Rowland. Rowland was made a minister of the Anglican Church in 1734 at Llangeitho, in Ceredigion. Yet he did not commit himself fully to Christ until he saw Griffith Jones preaching the following year.

The effect was dramatic, and the previously worldly Rowland became a committed Christian, developing connections with Nonconformists to more effectively spread the word. His preaching skills became legendary, and thousands came from all over Wales to his sermons at Llangeitho Church.

As a consequence the Anglican authorities became alarmed and expelled him from his position as curate. His followers responded by building him a chapel a short distance from the church and Rowland carried on as before, becoming one of the most influential preachers Wales ever produced.

William Williams ('Pantycelyn') was the great hymnwriter of the revival, composing almost a thousand hymns in both Welsh and English. His most famous English hymn is the rugby favourite 'Guide Me Oh Thou Great Redeemer'. Such was his talent he acquired the nickname Y Per Ganiedydd ('The Sweet Singer'). He also wrote prose and poetry.

From a Nonconformist background, Williams was converted by the preaching of Howel Harris, and later developed a close working relationship with Daniel Rowland. After joining the Anglican Church he was ordained deacon in 1740. Later he concentrated more on the Methodist movement and was to become one of the prominent figures in Wales. He travelled thousands of miles, preaching and selling his hymnbooks, and supported himself by selling goods such as tea.

Most hymnwriters of this period were men, but Ann Griffiths (1776-1805) was an exception to the rule. One of her admirers is the present Archbishop of Canterbury, Dr Rowan Williams . As part of his enthronement service as Archbishop of Canterbury in February 2003, Dr Williams chose (and translated himself) one of Ann Griffiths' hymns, 'Yr Arglwydd Iesu' (The Lord Jesus' or 'I Saw Him Standing'). Also included was Pantycelyn's hymn 'Guide Me Oh Thou Great Redeemer'.

The birth of nonconformity

Religious freedom for dissent was accompanied by a steady rise in literacy, which prepared the way for massive changes.

The Toleration Act of 1689 finally allowed religious freedom to the hard core of Dissenters who had come into existence during the time of Oliver Cromwell. They defiantly adhered to their beliefs during the years of persecution following the restoration.

The first chapels in Wales were built during this period, with one of the most famous examples being Maes-yr-Onnen near Glasbury, Powys.

Much of the development of Dissent was possible because of the steady rise in literacy. This was given a boost by the 1650 Act for the Better Propagation and Preaching of the Gospel. Before the Toleration Act there were increasing numbers of religious books available. In Welsh, notable books published during the 1680s were Canwyll y Cymry ('The Welshman's Candle') by the Vicar Prichard, and the first Welsh translation of 'The Pilgrim's Progress' by John Bunyan. The last work in particular was to be very influential on prominent figures in the Methodist revival later in the 18th century.

Educational opportunities were growing in this period thanks to the work of bodies like the Welsh Trust . Set up by Thomas Gouge following an illegal preaching tour of Wales in 1671, the Trust endeavoured to tackle the disturbing levels of illiteracy and general destitution then existing.

Initially working in English, following the influence of Puritan Stephen Hughes, the Trust made available Welsh translations of the Catechism, the book of Psalms and the Book of Common Prayer. This was made possible due to the financial patronage of, amongst others, the Lord Mayor of London.

However the Trust was active for only a short time. Soon a new body was established to carry on the work, to be known as the Society for the Promotion of Christian Knowledge. The SPCK faced a serious problem with the shortage of teachers for its schools, a problem compounded by the fact that the teaching was in the medium of English whilst the majority of pupils were first language Welsh speakers.

Griffith Jones was a Welsh clergyman working for the SPCK who became very dissatisfied with the sole use of English in the important cause of saving Welsh souls, and he decided to do something about it. With the help of Carmarthenshire heiress and philanthropist Madam Bevan he set up circulating schools to teach elementary reading and writing skills. These schools were very successful in making a large section of the Welsh people literate. Established in the early 1730s, it has been estimated that the schools succeeded in teaching some 200,000 people basic reading and writing skills, out of an approximate population of some 450,000.

After Griffith Jones' death in 1761 Madam Bevan ensured the continuation of the schools. The Empress of Russia, Catherine the Great, was sufficiently impressed by the results of these schools to commission a report in 1764.

This increase in literacy undoubtedly helped pave the way for the momentous events of the latter part of the 18th century, when Wales experienced the Methodist Revival.

Kelvin Gordon

Industrialisation & temperance

Government reports on Wales portrayed a country of ignorance and moral laxity. The patriotic backlash was a boost for Nonconformity and its values.

Following the public disturbances in Wales during the 1830s and 1840s the government commissioned a number of reports, the most famous of which was an examination of the education system. Popularly known as the Blue Books, it resulted in uproar when it was published in 1847.

The report contained a number of valid points but it was weakened by the fact it had been carried out by three English lawyers who had little or no previous knowledge of Wales and its native language.

As well as noting the deficiencies in the provision of education in the country, it also contained material critical of the Welsh language as well as the morals of the Welsh people.

The report became part of the intense religious debate taking place in the country between the Nonconformist and the established Church. It was portrayed by some Nonconformists as a direct Anglican attack on the Welsh people and their culture, a charge which was unfair to say the least.

There were patriotic Anglicans in Wales who also attacked the report for its faults, yet the fevered atmosphere caused contributed to the general impression that the Church of England was an 'alien' presence in the country.

Alien or not, in 1851 the only religious census in this country showed that Anglican worshippers in Wales were in the minority - most Christians were by then Nonconformist.

The Industrial Revolution was proceeding apace. The first wave of industrialism was built upon metal, such as iron and copper works. But by the middle of the nineteenth century coal mining was beginning to take off as the fuel demand for furnaces, railways and steamships began to rise.

It is no coincidence that all this activity was taking place at the same time as the British Empire was expanding and acquiring new territories and resources. These factors led to Wales becoming one of the first countries to have a majority of its people working in industry, a development of crucial importance to Welsh politics right down to the present day.

People flooded into the valleys of south Wales to find work, creating new communities in the process. As new pits were sunk, new chapels were rising in the industrial areas at a quicker rate than Anglican churches. As a consequence Nonconformity was to leave a particular stamp on the culture of Wales, particularly in these valley towns.

Alcohol was a particular bugbear of the chapels in these areas, and a sustained period of campaigning saw the passing of the Sunday Closing Act in 1881. The measure to close pubs on the Sabbath was one of the few pieces of legislation of the period which referred only to Wales, so Nonconformity can be shown to have contributed to the growing distinctiveness of the country.

Yet not all patriots would raise a glass to its passing since it was one of the measures that gave religion, particularly in the Welsh language, such a killjoy image. This was to rebound spectacularly on both Nonconformity and the language much later on in the next century, but in the meantime the forces of temperance were to enjoy a huge influence over the next hundred years.

Chapels became the centres of cultural activity in these new towns, and much of the tradition of Welsh choral singing dates from this period. This was helped by the introduction of the Sol-fa musical system which enabled large numbers of people to take an active part in choir singing. A major motive in encouraging music making was to keep people out of the pubs.

Culture & politics

Chapel democracy gave Welsh Nonconformity a voice, and Disestablishment of the Anglican Church became a controversial political issue.

Nonconformity was based upon democratic principles . Individual members were consulted on how their chapels were organised, in contrast with the more hierarchical nature of the Church. Debate was part and parcel of chapel life, and fuelled by the principles of their religion and aided by increasing literacy in Welsh and English, members would also discuss the great issues of the day.

The 1884 Reform Act meant that most men now had the vote (although women had to wait until 1918), and the Nonconformists were now in a position to start flexing some political muscle.

A Methodist deacon from Denbigh, north east Wales, saw the potential. His name was to become famous all over Wales thanks to his publishing business, Gwasg Gee. Thomas Gee used it to help the Nonconformist cause, and his most famous publication, the weekly/bi-weekly newspaper 'Baner ac Amserau Cymru', acquired a campaigning, radical reputation.

One cause in particular became a familiar theme in the paper - the campaign to disestablish the Church of England in Wales.

The fact that Anglicans in Wales still enjoyed legal privileges in Wales over the Nonconformist majority struck Gee and many others, as grossly unfair. The issue became particularly bitter when violence broke out over the issue of tithes.

A tithe was a traditional payment which entitled the Church to a tenth of people's annual income, which it was entitled to claim whether or not a person went to Church. With Wales a predominantly chapel going country, confrontation was inevitable and took place all across the country.

One of the most violent episodes happened in 1886-90 in Gee's own area. Dubbed 'The Tithe Wars' in the press, the disturbances involved enraged Denbighshire farm labourers having running battles with the local police over the issue, leading eventually to the deployment of a troop of lancers to protect the tithe collectors in carrying out their unpopular duties.

An Anti-Tithe League was formed to campaign across the country, and in south Caernarfonshire its secretary was a young solicitor named David Lloyd George.

By 1890 he was in Parliament as MP for Caernarfon. He was one of a number of young Liberal MPs who seemed to embody the particular values of Welsh Nonconformity. The feeling that the political home of Welsh Nonconformity was to be in the Liberal party was confirmed after a parliamentary speech by the great Liberal leader, William Gladstone. During a debate he stated that "The Nonconformists of Wales are the people of Wales".

However, hopes for disestablishment were dashed following the defeat of the Liberals in the 1895 election. The Tory administration put the issue on the back burner, and by the time the Liberals were returned to power other issues had come to prominence.

The issue was finally resolved in 1920 when the Church in Wales was established with its own Archbishop to officially represent Anglicanism in

Wales. But before that happened, the country experienced both a Great Revival and the Great War.

The Revival

The 'land of revivals' experienced the biggest one to date as Evan Roberts swept through Wales, converting thousands to the gospel.

From the middle of the 18th century to the middle of the 19th, Wales experienced some 15 major revivals, resulting in its reputation as 'the land of revivals'. The last great revival of this period had been in 1859, and although there was much local religious activity during the remainder of the 19th century, many people were wondering when, and if, the next great national one would happen.

When the revival did finally occur, it proved to be the biggest that the country had ever experienced. It seems to have its roots in southern Cardiganshire, where there were a number of meetings of religious leaders actively working on a revival. But when it did finally erupt, it became identified with one man in particular, an ex-collier from Loughor in western Glamorgan named Evan Roberts.

Roberts had begun to study for the ministry, and following a number of religious experiences during 1904, he had a revelation during a prayer meeting. This took place in Newcastle Emlyn, in the area of Cardiganshire where there had been a lot of work to prepare the way for a revival. He said, "I felt ablaze with a desire to go through the length and breadth of Wales to tell of the Saviour."

Shortly afterwards in the autumn of 1904 he first took the message with him back to his home chapel, Moriah, in Loughor, and following the ecstatic response he took it to other parts of Wales. The last great revival had begun.

Thousands of meetings occurred during the revival, from the southern valleys to Anglesey and north east Wales. Although Roberts garnered the headlines, preaching at around 200 meetings, there were also thousands of meetings led by other preachers held right across the country.

During those tumultuous months scarcely any aspect of Welsh life remained untouched. Work in various coalmines and metal works started with a prayer, and leisure activities like eisteddfodau, amateur dramatics and sport suffered a drop in support. A number of rugby clubs were disbanded by their members, who on receiving the message now felt rugby was an activity not compatible with being a true Christian. And it goes without saying that pubs and taverns saw a fall in consumption of the demon drink.

The up and coming politician, David Lloyd George, was caught up in the fervour. He said the movement was "rocking Welsh life like a Great Earthquake."

Even children began organising their own religious meetings, and communal hymn singing ('Cymanfa Ganu'), Bible reading and Temperance were now the favoured activities of many people across the country.

As a result, chapel building received a boost. Singing in particular had a prominent place, echoing the prophetic words of the famous musician Joseph Parry (composer of the love song 'Myfanwy') who said that "the next revival will be a singing revival."

Part of the appeal of the revival lay in Evan Roberts himself, a charismatic and sincere preacher. Although he came from the Welsh Methodist tradition, he wasn't a theologian, and he never finished his training to be a minister. His message was for all the people of Wales, regardless of denomination, and it was immensly appealing. Meetings would be a mixture of prayer, self examination and singing, and they could last for hours.

His mission was closely followed by the daily press, particularly the Western Mail, and the intervention of the media was something unique to this particular revival. Roberts become something of a personality, with his picture regularly in the papers as well as being featured on postcards. In today's terms he has been labelled a 'spiritual David Beckham'. According to one historian, a cynical interpretation might label the whole episode as an early exercise in press hype.

By the middle of 1905 the Revival was all but over and Roberts left Wales for a number of years. He eventually returned and died in 1951, to be buried in his chapel, Moriah. He is acknowledged by many Christians as the first charismatic leader of the 20th century, and among his legacies is the Apostolic

Church, whose founders were inspired by this great revival.

During this time socialism was getting established with the founding of trade unions and socialist societies. One of its first MPs, Keir Hardie, was elected in 1900 to represent Merthyr Tydfil, and this new philosophy would threaten and eventually shatter the old Liberal and Nonconformist consensus which had effectively governed Wales since the late 19th century. The Wales that emerged from the cataclysm of the First World War was a very different country from the one that experienced the fervour of the young Evan Roberts.

Kelvin Gordon

The growth of secularism

The First World War saw a collapse of the old order across Europe, and in Wales organised Christianity went into a long decline.

Lloyd George's promise after World War I to create a land fit for heroes rang hollow in many people's lives. The carnage of the war led to a questioning of the old certainties, and developments in politics, education and the media reflected this change. The word of God was no longer unchallenged at a popular level. Darwin's explosive theory regarding the origins of mankind had been around for fifty years, and the Bible's account of creation was now a matter of everyday debate.

Young socialists like Aneurin Bevan in Tredegar rejected the beliefs of their Nonconformist parents in favour of the promise of Socialism.

The chill winds of the depression from the mid 1920s onwards saw a fight back from Christians who wanted to act on their principles and actively do something to improve the living conditions of people, particularly in the poverty-stricken valleys of south east Wales. Christian Socialism's founding father was the 19th century philanthropist Robert Owen, from Newtown in Powys.

Robert Owen's principles inspired a new wave of Christian activity in the valleys. In Tonypandy the Wesleyan minister Rex Barker opened a famous social centre in the town's Central Hall. In 1936 he wrote an influential book based on his experiences, 'Christ In The Valley of Unemployment'. Also in the Rhondda the Quakers established another social centre at Trealaw, called Maes-yr-Haf.

These good works among others are testament to the good intentions and deeds of committed Christians, but their efforts were dwarfed by the sheer scale of the suffering at that time.

The Second World War finally kick-started the Welsh economy by increasing the demand for coal and the building of munitions factories to serve the war effort, but both the war and the immediate post war world proved to be another kick in the teeth for religion. Newsreels showed cinema audiences the horrors of the war, and although Christians responded by arguing that war was an act of man, popular sympathy was not on their side.

Peacetime brought further benefits of the material world. The coming of the car increased mobility. No longer were people confined to their communities on the Sabbath, with no choice apart from going to chapel three times. Now they could drive to the seaside, or visit whoever they wanted. They weren't limited, whereas chapel life seemed to be restricting.

Dylan Thomas''bible-black' phrase from 'Under Milk Wood' neatly captures the dour image of religion, as does the famous quote of the Rhondda writer Gwyn Thomas- "There are still parts of Wales where the only concession to gaiety is a striped shroud."

The existence of the Sunday Closing act in parts of Wales down to the 1990s also continued the impression of a culture that liked to say no more often than it said yes to the simple pleasures of life. The arrival of the 'permissive society' in Wales sometime in the 1970s was to be bad news for this particular way of life. These new freethinkers had little time for the severity of the chapels, and this happened at a time when the last great generation of chapel goers was starting to die off.

As they were not being replaced by new recruits, chapels began to close down. Some were converted to new uses such as homes, shops, even an adult film cinema. Others were simply left to rot.

The 2001 Census shows that today in Wales fewer than one in ten people regularly attend a church or chapel, slightly lower than the figures for Scotland and England. However, it also shows that over 70% of Welsh people see themselves as Christian, perhaps demonstrating that while they don't actively worship God, their lives are still strongly influenced by Christian values and principles. And that is not really surprising in historic terms, because one of the defining characteristics of the Welsh is the Christian religion.

This particular legacy of the Roman Empire, combined with the language, differentiated the Welsh from the invading Germanic pagan tribes of over 1,500 years ago. Therefore, if Christianity does die out in Wales, the question arises as to what kind of country Wales will be.

It cannot be denied that Christianity has made an important contribution to the development of Wales since its arrival in Britain almost two thousand years ago. And if it is correct to say that the future of Christianity in Wales is unknowable, then it is equally correct to say that the history of Wales is unknowable without a proper acknowledgement and respect of its Christian origins.

Kelvin Gordon

Multicultural Wales

All the major world religions have a presence all across Wales, some of which have been represented for many years.

Wales has a number of ethnic communities, many of whose members belong to non-Christian faiths. They are to be found mainly in the cities of Cardiff, Swansea and Newport. All the world's major religions are present in the country, such as Judaism, Islam, Buddhism, Hinduism and Sikhism. Cardiff boasts the highest proportion of members of most of these religions.

The oldest non-Christian faith to be established was Judaism , with a presence in Swansea dating from around 1730. Jewish communities were formed in the next century in Cardiff, Merthyr Tydfil, Pontypridd and Tredegar. 1911 was a year of industrial disputes and public disorder in Wales with major riots in Tonypandy and Llanelli. In August of that year, Jewish shops across the south Wales coalfield were targeted and attacked by mobs. As a result the Jewish population declined in these areas, leaving only Cardiff with a sizeable Jewish community. Blame for the attacks have been attributed to contemporary anti-Semitic undertones existing in both early socialist propaganda and Welsh Nonconformity. At its height in around 1913, it is thought that the total number of Jews was around 4,000 to 5,000, which by the 2001 Census had declined to about 2,000.

The largest non-Christian faith in Wales is also the fastest growing faith in the world today, which is Islam . In the 2001 Census it had 22,000 members. Many Muslims came to south Wales during Cardiff's heyday as the largest coal exporting port in the world and by now they are well established. It is thought that the Yemenis of the city are the oldest Muslim community in Britain, dating from the mid to late 19th Century. The first purpose-built mosque was erected in Cardiff in 1947 and the following year Cardiff hosted Britain's first ever Muslim conference.

Wales has about 40 mosques, most of which are in Cardiff, with others in Newport, Swansea and Haverfordwest. A college for training Muslim clerics has been established in Llanybydder in west Wales.

Hinduism has around 5,000 Welsh members, the same number as Buddhism. The largest proportion of Buddhists is to be found in Ceredigion.

Sikhism has around 2,000 members and the first purpose-built Sikh gurdwara was opened in Cardiff in 1989.

The 2001 Census shows that 'Other Religions' in Wales numbered some 7,000 members. Amongst that number are a large number of pagans, including those who see themselves as Druids. These modern day Druids base their beliefs on numerous sources, including ancient Welsh literature. This revival of a form of Druidism arguably marks a full circle in the history of religion in Wales, as it brings the story back to the beliefs that were practised before the Romans invaded.

This form of Druidism should not be confused with the 'Gorsedd y Beirdd', familiar to many from the Nationa Eisteddfod. The 'Gorsedd' is a cultural body, concerned primarily with promoting and maintaining the Welsh language. There were a lot of newspaper headlines about its 'pagan' origins when the Archbishop of Canterbury, Rowan Williams , was admitted as a member in 2002.

Perhaps a worrying trend for the religions of Wales may be the fact revealed in the 2001 Census that over half a million people in Wales now profess to have no religion whatsoever. That accounts for around one in six of the population.

There is nothing new in the arrival of new religions to Wales. After all, many years ago Christianity itself was a strange, exotic religion before it put down roots and made itself at home. The reality is that Wales, like the other countries of the UK, is now home to many faiths.

Indeed, Prince Charles has acknowledged this by floating the idea that on becoming king he would like the old title 'Defender of the Faith', inherited from the days of Henry VIII, amended to 'Defender of Faiths'. His remarks have been welcomed as indicating a more inclusive approach to religion, although they have also drawn some flak from traditionalists.

The ensuing debate shows that although organised religion may be in decline, faith is still very much a live topic and very much tied up with how people define themselves. Religion in Wales, in all its different guises, is not going to go away just yet.

www.ingramcontent.com/pod-product-compliance
Lightning Source LLC
Chambersburg PA
CBHW021122080526
44587CB00010B/605